P9-DFJ-164

Atlantic Gourmet

THE BEST OF ICELANDIC SEAFOOD

Atlantic Gourmet

THE BEST OF ICELANDIC SEAFOOD

Iceland Review

Atlantic Gourmet
© Bjarni Thór Ólafsson, 1997
Photographs: Gudmundur Ingólfsson
English translation: Anna Yates
Design: Erlingur Páll Ingvarsson og Hildigunnur Gunnarsdóttir
Lithography: Prentmyndastofan hf., Reykjavík
Printed in Italy
Published by Iceland Review © Reykjavík, Iceland 1997

All rights reserved. No part of this publication may be reproduced,
stored in a retrieval system, or transmitted in any form or by any
means, electronic, mechanical, photocopying, recording or other-
wise, without the permission of the publishers.

ISBN 9979-51-121-4

CONTENTS

PREFACE

As with all countries, Iceland has its own culinary specialities, and not surprisingly for an island nation, one speciality is seafood.

The variety and quality of catch from the chill and pristine waters of the Atlantic Ocean, and fresh-tasting fish from the country's crystal-clear lakes and rivers, is a source of national pride.

Today, the choice of seafood and fish is so much more than it was just a few decades ago, and the diversity of raw material has led to still more imagination when it comes to preparation. People have discovered new and creative ways to present the healthy and delicious fresh-water catches and the fruits of the sea, much to the admiration and satisfaction of the countless visitors to Iceland each year.

Many have dreamt of returning home and preparing similar dishes in their own kitchens. And since Icelandic seafood is now widely available around the world, that dream can become a reality.

This book presents twenty five simple and easy-to-follow recipes for first and main courses featuring Icelandic seafood and fish. Careful consideration has been given in their selection to ensure that the full essence and qualities of the ingredients will be brought out.

Now anyone can create a memorable meal featuring the best of what Iceland has to offer!

STARTERS

Prawn soup with a lid of puff pastry

For 4

750 ml prawn stock
3 tbsp butter
$^1/_2$ leek, finely chopped
2 cloves garlic, finely chopped
2 tsp curry powder
2 dl white wine
5 dl cream
corn flour
salt and pepper
200 g prawns, peeled
ready-made puff pastry, rolled out to a thickness of 3 mm
1 egg, beaten

Prawn stock

Heat 15 prawns (in the shell) in oil, together with 1 finely-chopped onion, 100 g carrots, thinly sliced, and 3 tbsp of tomato purée (paste). Add 1 litre of water. Simmer for 20 minutes, then strain through muslin.

Melt the butter in a saucepan, and cook the leek, garlic and curry powder in the butter for 3 minutes. Add the prawn stock and white wine, and simmer for 10 minutes. Add the cream, and cook for 4 minutes. Thicken the liquid with corn flour, stirred into a little cold water, and season with salt and pepper. Leave the soup to cool.

Pour into four bowls, add the prawns, then cut circles of puff pastry that generously cover the tops of the bowls. Brush the edges of the bowls with whipped egg, and place the puff pastry on top, pressing the edges down. Brush the dough lids carefully with egg. Bake in the oven at 180°C for 15 minutes.

Prawns with courgettes, saffron and garlic

For 4

600 g large prawns (shell-on weight),
  raw, peeled except for the tail
6 tbsp olive oil
100 g courgette (zucchini), sliced
6 cloves garlic, finely chopped
1 tsp marjoram
$^1/_2$ tsp saffron
2 tomatoes, peeled and cut into cubes
2 dl white wine
salt and pepper

Heat the olive oil in a pan, and sautée the prawns for 2 minutes. Season with salt and pepper, then transfer the prawns to a dish and keep them hot. Sautée the courgette (zucchini) slices, and season with garlic, marjoram, saffron, salt and pepper. Add the tomatoes and white wine. Simmer for 2 minutes. Serve on four plates.

*P*âté of lumpfish caviar served with Dijon dressing

For 4

50 g lumpfish caviar
150 g salmon roe
50 g smoked salmon, finely chopped
2 dl crème fraîche (sour cream)
1 dl sparkling wine
2 tbsp parsley, chopped
2 tbsp fresh green dill, chopped
8 sheets gelatine, soaked in cold water
juice of 1 lemon
salt and pepper

Mix the sparkling wine thoroughly with the crème fraîche (sour cream), then add the lumpfish caviar, salmon roe, smoked salmon, and herbs. Carefully melt the gelatine in the water over a low heat, and add to the mixture. Season with lemon juice, salt and pepper. Pour the mixture into four moulds, and chill for 3 hours in the refrigerator.

Dijon dressing

1 dl crème fraîche (sour cream)
¹/₂ dl mayonnaise
1 tsp Dijon mustard
1 tsp lemon juice
2 cloves garlic, finely chopped
salt and pepper

Mix all the ingredients together, and season with salt and pepper to taste.

Cod roe with avocado and prawns served with lemon dressing

For 4

100 g cod roe
260 g prawns, peeled
1 avocado, ripe, peeled and cut into chunks
1 red onion, finely chopped
fresh dill

Mix the prawns with the avocado, place in well-chilled bowls, and pour the lemon dressing over them. Top with roe and red onion, and garnish with dill.

Lemon dressing

juice of 1 lemon
2 tbsp oil
salt and fresh-ground pepper

Mix all the ingredients together in a bowl.

Juniper-cured salmon served with mustard-walnut dressing

For 4

400 g salmon, filleted
80 g salt
50 g sugar
20 juniper berries, coarsely ground
10 freeze-dried green peppercorns, coarsely ground
¹/₂ dl olive oil

Mix the salt with the sugar, juniper berries and peppercorns. Brush the salmon with the oil, coat with the juniper mixture, and leave to stand in the refrigerator for 48 hours.

Mustard-walnut dressing

50 g dark mustard
50 g sweet mustard
20 g Dijon mustard
1 tbsp soft brown sugar
2 tbsp fresh green dill
3 tbsp coarsely chopped walnuts
4 tbsp walnut oil

Combine all the ingredients and mix thoroughly.

Smoked river trout with almonds served with herb dressing

For 4

400 g smoked river trout (or other smoked trout)
30 g honey
6 tbsp flaked almonds
juice of ¹/₂ a lemon

Heat the honey in a saucepan with the almonds and lemon juice, then pour over the smoked trout, and leave to stand in the refrigerator for 4 hours.

Herb dressing

2 tbsp green dill, finely chopped
2 tbsp parsley, finely chopped
3 tbsp chives, finely chopped
1 ¹/₂ dl crème fraîche (sour cream)
¹/₂ dl mayonnaise
lemon juice
salt and pepper

Mix the crème fraîche (sour cream) with the mayonnaise, and add the herbs. Mix thoroughly. Season to taste with salt, pepper and lemon juice.

Scallop and bacon kebabs served with port sauce

For 4

24 scallops, large
8 slices bacon
8 bamboo kebab pins
200 g leek, cut into julienne strips

Wrap each scallop in a strip of bacon, then thread onto bamboo kebab pins. Briefly fry the scallops in a frying pan with the leek for 3 minutes. Pour the sauce onto a hot dish, add the scallop kebabs and the leek.

Port sauce

3 shallot onions, finely chopped
3 slices bacon, finely chopped
2 dl port
1 dl white wine
25 g butter
salt and pepper

Heat the bacon and shallot onion in the butter. Add the port and white wine, and boil until reduced to half. Add butter to thicken the sauce. Season with salt and pepper to taste.

Marinated lobster with caviar dressing

For 4 | **350 g lobster meat (out of the shell)**

Marinade

1 dl olive oil
1 dl white wine
1 tbsp brandy
¹/₂ leek, finely chopped
¹/₂ red pepper (capsicum), finely chopped
¹/₂ green pepper (capsicum), finely chopped
1 tbsp lemon pepper
juice of 1 lemon

Mix all the ingredients together and pour over the lobster meat. Leave to stand in the refrigerator for 2 hours.

Sautée the lobster meat in a frying pan for 1-2 minutes, and leave to cool. Serve the lobster with the caviar dressing.

Caviar dressing

1 dl crème fraîche (sour cream)
¹/₂ dl mayonnaise
¹/₂ dl cream
10 freeze-dried green peppercorns
¹/₂ onion, finely chopped
1 tbsp white wine
1 tbsp brandy
1 tsp Dijon mustard
20 g cooked prawns, finely chopped
2 tbsp prawn stock
4 tbsp red lumpfish caviar
fresh-ground pepper

Thoroughly mix all the ingredients together.

MAIN COURSES

$\mathcal{B}$aked Arctic charr with vegetables

For 4

8 small fillets Arctic charr (or small trout), bones removed
1 dl white wine
80 g butter
salt and pepper

Arrange the fish fillets on a baking tray, season with salt and pepper, top with the vegetable mixture, and add the white wine and pats of butter. Bake in the oven at 180°C for 8 minutes.

Vegetables

1 red onion, chopped
3 tbsp parsley, chopped
2 tbsp dill, chopped
2 tbsp lemon balm, chopped
3 tbsp chives, chopped
4 tbsp carrots, thinly sliced
4 tbsp red pepper (capsicum), cut in julienne strips
4 tbsp leek, sliced

Arctic charr en croûte with lime sauce

For 4

650 g Arctic charr fillets, skin and bones removed, cut into four equal portions
8 sheets filo pastry
60 g mushrooms, sliced
4 tbsp leek, sliced
60 g blue cheese, grated
juice of a lemon
80 g butter
salt and pepper

Take two sheets of filo pastry, place the fish portion on top, and season with salt and pepper. Add mushrooms, leek and a pat of butter, and then the lemon juice and blue cheese. Lift up the four corners of the dough, and press them together in the centre. Melt the remainder of the butter, and brush the outside of each dough "parcel" with the melted butter. Bake in the oven at 180°C for 7 minutes. Serve with the sauce and fried tomatoes or vegetable.

Lime sauce

¹/₂ onion, finely chopped
25 g butter
1 dl white wine
juice of two limes
finely grated peel of a lime
1 dl cream
salt and pepper

Heat the butter in a saucepan, and heat the onion in it. Add the white wine and lime juice and peel. Simmer for 5 minutes to reduce. Add the cream, season with salt and pepper, and simmer for 4 minutes.

Baked salmon with cheese served with lemon-thyme sauce

For 4

780 g salmon, skin and bones removed, cut into four portions
120 g Lymeswold or other soft blue cheese
finely grated peel of 2 lemons
3 tbsp fresh thyme
salt and fresh-ground pepper
160 g butter, cut into small pieces
juice of two lemons

Brown the fish in butter in a frying pan for 3 minutes each side, and season with salt and pepper. Arrange the fish portions in an ovenproof dish, and add slices of cheese. Bake in the oven at 170°C for 8 minutes.

Meanwhile, heat the lemon peel and thyme in butter in a pan over a low heat. Pour the lemon juice into the pan, and stir in the butter, cut into small pieces. Serve the salmon with the sauce, potatoes and vegetable.

Salmon-halibut duet with saffron sauce

For 4

480 g **halibut fillets,** skin and bones removed
480 g **salmon fillets,** skin and bones removed
120 g **butter**
5 dl **white wine**
½ **onion,** finely chopped
pinch of saffron
3 dl **cream**
salt

Cut the fish fillets into sections 10 cm long, then into strips 2 cm wide, lengthways along the fish. Plait together four strips of salmon and four of halibut, then place the fish plaits on a well-greased frying pan, season with salt, add the white wine, and steam with the lid on for 6 minutes.

Meanwhile, heat the onion in the butter, together with the saffron, over a low heat. Add the fish stock, stir well, then add the cream and season to taste. Can be served with fried vegetable on filo pastry.

Fried halibut with rosemary, garlic and chilli

For 4

800 g halibut, cut into 8 equal portions
2 dl flour
6 tbsp oil
$^1/_4$ tsp red chilli flakes
2 tbsp parsley, finely chopped
2 tbsp fresh rosemary, coarsely chopped
1 tbsp garlic, finely chopped
juice of 2 lemons
3 tbsp white-wine vinegar
salt and pepper

Coat the fish in the flour, heat the oil in a pan, fry the fish, and season with salt and pepper. After about 3 minutes each side, remove the fish from the pan, and keep it hot. Add the chilli flakes, parsley, rosemary and garlic to the pan, and heat. Add the lemon juice and white-wine vinegar. Simmer for 4 minutes. Add the fish, and simmer for another 2 minutes. Place the fish on a hot dish, and pour the liquid over it. Serve with vegetable.

$\int$ teamed halibut with snails and fennel sauce

For 4

780 g halibut, skin and bones removed
1 dl white wine
2 tbsp fresh fennel, finely chopped
2 tbsp red pepper (capsicum), finely chopped
1 tbsp onion, finely chopped
1 can (300 ml) snails (escargots)
3 tbsp Pernod
2 dl cream
1 tsp dried fennel
salt and pepper

Cut the halibut in eight equal portions, and steam for 4 minutes with the white wine, fennel, red pepper (capsicum) and onion, seasoned with salt and pepper. Remove the fish from the pan and keep it hot.

Add the Pernod, snails and cream, and season with dried fennel if desired. Boil to reduce until the sauce has thickened sufficiently. Pour the sauce over the fish.

Baked redfish with fennel tomatoes

For 4

700 g redfish, skin and bones removed, cut into 4 equal portions
4 tbsp olive oil
1 onion, sliced
1 can tomatoes (without juice)
1 dl white wine
peel of 2 oranges, cut into narrow strips
$^1/_2$ tsp fennel seed
$^1/_2$ tsp chilli powder
salt and pepper

Heat 2 tbsp of oil in a pan, and heat the onion for 4 minutes. Add the tomatoes, white wine, orange peel, fennel seed and chilli powder. Simmer for 10 minutes over a low heat.

Pour 2 tbsp of oil into an ovenproof dish, arrange the fish pieces in the dish, and season with salt and pepper. Pour the hot sauce over the fish, and bake at 150°C for 15 minutes.

Plaice stuffed with asparagus served with chive-egg sauce

For 4

700 g plaice, skin and bones removed, cut into 8 equal portions
1 can (350 g) green asparagus
1 ½ dl white wine
80 g butter
30 g chives, chopped
salt and pepper

Thoroughly grease a pan. Arrange the plaice fillets with the skin side up, and season with salt and pepper. Place the asparagus across each fillet, and roll them up attractively. Arrange the rolls on the greased pan, season with salt, pepper and chives, add the white wine and simmer with the lid on for 6 minutes over a low heat. Meanwhile, make the sauce. Serve with vegetable.

Chive-egg sauce

200 g unsalted butter
3 egg yolks
2 tbsp water
salt and pepper
juice of ½ a lemon

Melt the butter, and skim off the froth with a spoon. Leave to cool until lukewarm. Whip the water and egg yolks together in a small saucepan, with a little salt and pepper, until thoroughly mixed, and light in colour. Place the pan over a low heat, and whip for 4 minutes. Remove the pan from the heat and whip in the lukewarm butter, a little at a time. Carefully add the liquid from the fish pan to the sauce, and then add the lemon juice.

Cod or Orange Roughy Wellington

For 4

600 g cod or orange roughy, skin and bones removed
80 g bread crumbs
1 tbsp thyme
1 tbsp basil
1 tbsp garlic powder
$^1/_2$ tbsp ginger
80 g butter
1 egg, beaten
salt and pepper

Ready-made puff pastry, rolled out to a thickness
of 3 mm, 12 cm x 12 cm
1 egg, beaten

Cut the fish into four equal portions. Mix the herbs and spices thoroughly with the bread crumbs. Coat the fish pieces thoroughly in egg, and then in the bread-crumb mixture. Fry in a pan in butter for 3 minutes each side. Leave the fish to cool.

Brush the edges of the puff pastry with egg, then place the fish portions on top. Fold the pastry over the fish, and press the ends down with a fork. Thoroughly brush the dough with egg. Bake in the oven at 180°C for 10 minutes.

*S*teamed cod or haddock with leek sauce

For 4

700 g cod or haddock fillets, skin and bones removed,
    cut into four equal portions
salt and pepper
0.2 dl dry white wine
1.4 dl fish stock

Steam the cod or haddock in the fish stock and white wine for 5 minutes, with the lid on. Arrange the fish on a dish, and serve with the sauce, potatoes and vegetable.

Leek sauce

0.6 dl dry white wine
0.6 dl fish stock
¹/₂ dl champagne vinegar
1¹/₂ dl cream
80 g butter
salt and fresh-ground pepper
100 g leek, sliced

Mix the white wine and the fish stock in a saucepan, and boil until reduced by half. Add the champagne vinegar, and cook for 3 minutes. Add the cream, and simmer over a low heat for 6 minutes. Then add the butter, a little at a time, and bring back to the boil. Season with salt and pepper. Heat the leek in butter, and add to the sauce.

Fried saithe or haddock with curried apple and onion

For 4

700 g saithe or haddock, skin and bones removed
1 tart apple (e.g. Granny Smith), peeled, cored and sliced
2 onions, sliced
3 tbsp curry powder
100 g butter
whole-wheat flour
salt and pepper

Coat the fish in the whole-wheat flour and season with salt and pepper. Melt 50 g butter in a pan, and fry the fish for 4 minutes each side, then remove the fish from the pan and keep it hot. Add the remainder of the butter to the pan, then the slices of apple and onion together with the curry powder. Fry for 4 minutes. Place the fish on a dish, and serve with the onion-apple mixture.

$\mathcal{L}$ing with mushrooms and tarragon cream sauce

For 4

700 g ling, skin and bones removed, cut into 4 equal portions
70 g butter
¹/₂ onion, finely chopped
200 g mushrooms, sliced
4 dl dry vermouth
2 dl cream
3 tsp fresh tarragon, coarsely chopped
salt and pepper

Melt the butter in a pan, and fry the onion and mushrooms for 3 minutes. Remove the mushrooms and onions from the pan, and put aside. Place the ling in the pan, pour the vermouth over the fish, and cook with the lid on for about 8 minutes. Remove the fish from the pan and keep it hot. Add the cream, simmer for 3 minutes, then add the mushrooms, onion and tarragon, and cook for another 3 minutes. Season to taste with salt and pepper. Pour the sauce over the ling, and serve with rice.

Fried wolf fish with Creole dressing

For 4

700 g wolf fish fillets, skin and bones removed, cut into 4 equal portions
3 tbsp olive oil
$^1/_2$ tsp fresh thyme, chopped
2 cloves garlic, finely chopped
juice of $^1/_2$ a lemon
salt and pepper

Heat the oil in a pan, and fry the fish for 4 minutes each side. Season with thyme, garlic, salt, pepper and lemon juice. Serve the cold Creole dressing with the fish.

Creole dressing

4 tbsp tomatoes, cut into chunks
3 tbsp olive oil
2 tbsp red onion, finely chopped
2 tbsp celery, chopped
2 tbsp carrots, chopped
2 tbsp red pepper (capsicum), chopped
2 tbsp chives, chopped
2 tbsp white-wine vinegar

Mix all the ingredients in a bowl, and leave to stand in the refrigerator for 3 hours.

Baked saltfish with tomatoes and potatoes

For 4

600 g saltfish (bacalao), soaked overnight in water, skin and bones removed, cut into 8 portions
5 tbsp water
150 g cooked potatoes, sliced
3 tbsp olive oil
1 onion, chopped
4 cloves garlic, finely chopped
1 can tomatoes, without juice, cut into chunks
1 tbsp fresh basil
salt and pepper
150 g grated Gouda or other mild cheese

Place the saltfish in a pan with the water, and steam with the lid on for 5 minutes. Transfer the fish to an ovenproof dish. Heat the olive oil in a pan, and heat the onion for 3 minutes. Add the garlic, tomato and basil, and season with salt and pepper. Arrange the potatoes with the saltfish, and pour the sauce over. Sprinkle grated cheese over the dish and bake in the oven at 160°C for 15 minutes.

*F*ried herring with nuts and sesame seed

For 4

8 fillets fresh herring
2 red onions, sliced
4 tbsp hazelnuts, chopped
4 tbsp sesame seed
1 egg, beaten
5 tbsp oil
juice of a lemon
salt and pepper

Mix the hazelnuts with the sesame seed. Coat the herring in egg, and then in the nut-sesame seed mixture. Heat the oil in a pan, and fry the herring for 3 minutes each side. Season with salt and pepper. Finally add the onion and fry briefly. Pour lemon juice over the fish and serve with potatoes.

Fresh mussels cooked in white wine

For 4

2 kg mussels (cleanse well before cooking, and discard any open shells)
4 dl white wine
2 onions, chopped
5 tbsp parsley, chopped
2 lemons, sliced
fresh-ground pepper

Place the mussels in a saucepan, then add the white wine, onion, parsley, lemon slices and pepper. Steam with the lid on until the mussel shells open. Serve with a whole-grain bread.

Mixed seafood with Camembert sauce

For 4

150 g **scallops**
150 g **angler fish,** skin and bones removed, cut into
   8 equal portions
150 g **lobster,** out of the shell
150 g **prawns**
90 g **butter**
1 small **red pepper (capsicum),** chopped into chunks
1 **green pepper (capsicum),** chopped into chunks
$^1/_2$ **leek,** chopped into chunks
4 tbsp **chopped parsley**
1 dl **white wine**
juice of a lemon
80 g **Camembert cheese,** ripe
4 dl **cream**
100 g **grated Gouda or other mild cheese**
salt and pepper

Briefly fry the scallops, lobster and angler fish in butter, season with salt and pepper, and remove from the pan. Sautée all the vegetables in butter in a pan for 2 minutes, then add the white wine, lemon juice and Camembert, and cook for 5 minutes. Add the cream, and boil until the sauce thickens sufficiently. Add the scallops, lobster, angler fish and prawns. Simmer for another 3 minutes. Place the fish and shellfish into bowls, and top with grated cheese. Grill for 6 minutes.

INDEX